The Belgian Army in World War I

R Pawly & P Lierneux • Illustrated by P Courcelle
Series editor Martin Windrow

First published in Great Britain in 2009 by Osprey Publishing,
Midland House, West Way, Botley, Oxford OX2 0PH, UK
443 Park Avenue South, New York, NY 10016, USA
Email: **info@ospreypublishing.com**

ISBN: 978 1 84603 448 0
PDF e-book ISBN 978 1 84603 893 8

Editor: Martin Windrow
Design: Melissa Orrom Swan, Oxford
Index by Alan Thatcher
Originated by PPS Grasmere Ltd
Printed in China through World Print Ltd.

09 10 11 12 13   10 9 8 7 6 5 4 3 2 1

A CIP catalogue record for this book is available from the British Library

FOR A CATALOGUE OF ALL BOOKS PUBLISHED BY
OSPREY MILITARY AND AVIATION PLEASE CONTACT:

North America:
Osprey Direct, c/o Random House Distribution Center
400 Hahn Road, Westminster, MD 21157
E-mail: **uscustomerservice@ospreypublishing.com**

All other regions:
Osprey Direct The Book Service Ltd, Distribution Centre, Colchester
Road, Frating Green, Colchester, Essex, CO7 7DW, UK
E-mail: **customerservice@ospreypublishing.com**

Osprey Publishing is supporting the Woodland Trust, the UK's leading
Woodland conservation charity, by funding the dedication of trees.

www.ospreypublishing.com

Artist's Note

OPPOSITE: **The Soldier King: born in Brussels in 1875,
Albert Léopold Clément Marie Meinrad succeeded his
uncle Leopold II as third King of the Belgians in December
1909. His refusal to permit the passage of German troops
through his country was followed by the German invasion;
in personal command of the Belgian Army, King Albert
delayed the German advance for long enough for France
to prepare for the Battle of the Marne (6–9 September
1914). In 1918, as commander of Army Group Flanders,
Albert led the final offensive from the Yser that liberated
occupied Belgium. Here he wears the khaki 1915 uniform
with the collar ranking of a lieutenant-general – two vertical
gold bars and three stars – though his coat collar hides the
foudre or thunderbolt symbol behind them; general officers'
patches were black velvet piped with crimson. Note also
the national lion-mask badge plate on the M1915 Adrian
helmet. A passionate alpinist, King Albert I died tragically
in a climbing accident at Marche les Dames in the
Ardennes region of Belgium in 1934. See also Plate A2.
(Author's collection)**

THE BELGIAN ARMY 1914–18

HISTORICAL BACKGROUND

The Kingdom of Belgium – bordered by the Netherlands (Holland) to the north, Germany and Luxemburg to the east, France to the south and the English Channel to the west – was only 84 years old when the Great War broke out. In 1814 the Congress of Vienna, redrawing the maps of Europe following Napoleon's first abdication, had created a Kingdom of the Netherlands under the Dutch King Willem I. This combination of the northern Protestant Netherlands, an independent nation for much of the previous 200 years, with the southern Catholic provinces, historically ruled by the Spanish and Austrian Habsburg empires, had proved unsustainable. In 1830 the Belgian Revolution resulted in the declaration of an independent and Catholic Belgian kingdom under the rule of King Leopold I. The independence and neutrality of this new state was generally in the interests of the great powers; by the Treaty of London (1839) the Netherlands recognized Belgium, and her neutrality was formally guaranteed by the Netherlands, France, England, Prussia, Russia and Austria. The young kingdom escaped the devastating Franco-Prussian War (1870–71); Belgium mobilized its army to protect its borders and neutrality, but in the event they only had to deal with French troops who crossed the frontier seeking refuge from capture by the Prussians. For the first time in many centuries, 'the battlefield of Europe' was not situated on Belgian territory.

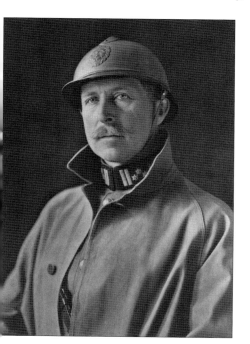

By the beginning of the 20th century this small but wealthy nation, with a population of just over 7 million, was an advanced industrial power and a participant in the colonization of Africa. In the event of another war between France and Germany the most explicit international treaties placed Belgium outside the conflict, and since the royal government scrupulously observed the agreements defining its international status it was convinced that the country was secure from invasion. However, this confidence did not blind Belgian governments to the increasing military preparations being made by neighbouring nations. King Leopold II (1865–1909) was supported in his arguments for military reforms by some able generals and politicians, notably Gen Brialmont (1821–1903), and the king signed on his deathbed the law of 14 December 1909 instituting compulsory military service by one son from each family. This reform did away with the old system by which the necessary quotas of recruits had been filled by lotteries; these had been open to many abuses, with

Antwerp, the 'National Redoubt', had been a well-fortified city with formidable walls and a citadel since the Spanish occupation; in the 1860s these were replaced by a first defence ring with massive monumental gates. In 1879 the brilliant engineer Alexis Brialmont was commissioned to design another ring of brick and masonry forts; between 1906 and 1913 both inner and outer forts received additional protection in reinforced concrete. Building these enormous constructions took so much time that they were outdated even before they were finished. (Author's collection)

prosperous families able to 'buy out' their sons by paying proxies from the poorer classes to serve in their place.

The political climate in continental Europe became increasingly inflamed, and without the steadying hand of old Bismarck to restrain the militarists surrounding the young Kaiser relations between France and Germany degenerated. On 17 May 1913 the Belgian Minister of War, de Broqueville, passed through both Chambers of Representatives a general military service law that aimed gradually to increase Belgian Army manpower to a total of 340,000.

THE MILITARY SITUATION IN 1914

In practice, even if the size of the army could indeed be tripled the country would still be far from prepared for a war against one of its giant neighbours, and the de Broqueville reforms had hardly come into application when Belgium was confronted by the chain of events leading to the outbreak of World War I. The army was still only 120,500 strong, of which 3,500 were gendarmes, and had a shortfall of 2,300 officers. In addition to this first-line strength it was planned that some 65,000 older men should serve in static fortress regiments, while the 46,000 members of the Civil Guard were intended mainly to maintain order and security in rear areas behind the lines.[1] Including mobilized reserves, the Belgian Army in August 1914 comprised the following first-line combat units:

Infantry:
14 regiments of the Line
3 regiments of Chasseurs á pied (light infantry)
1 Grenadier regiment
1 regiment of Carabiniers (Rifles) and 1 battalion of
   Carabinier-Cyclists
Corps of Gendarmerie
Cavalry:
2 regiments of Guides
3 regiments of Chasseurs á cheval (Mounted Rifles)
5 regiments of Lancers
Artillery:
3 Field regiments
2 Horse groups
3 Fortress groups
Engineers:
1 regiment

These units were organized into a Field Army of 120,500 troops and 18,000 volunteers. This was divided into 6 large Army Divisions each with between 25,000 and 32,000 men. Each division consisted of either 2 or 3

---

1 In addition to these figures, in the event the Germans would also be confronted by some 37,800 new recruits and civilian volunteers who rallied spontaneously during the first weeks of the August 1914 invasion.

In the 19th and early 20th century most visitors to Holland and Belgium expressed surprise when they first saw dogs used as beasts of burden; in these countries small carts drawn by large dogs were common – for instance, milk carts in every Belgian town. They were regularly used by the Belgian Army for light transport, such as the movement of machine guns by this unit of Carabiniers. At left, note NCOs' sleeve stripes. (Langley Collection, Antwerp)

Another angle on a column of Carabiniers on the march, with dog-carts loaded with machine-gun ammunition; the leafy branches are to keep the dogs cool in the sun rather than to camouflage them. Note also the horse-drawn ambulances. (Langley Collection, Antwerp)

brigades; each brigade had 2 infantry regiments (of 3 battalions) and one machine-gun company (with 6x Maxim or Hotchkiss guns). The divisional artillery consisted of 3 field batteries, each with 4x 75mm Tir Rapide Krupp guns, and a group of divisional horse artillery. The divisional cavalry regiment might be either Mounted Rifles or Lancers, and an aeronautical section had one or two Belgian-made Maurice Farman aircraft (which were subsequently removed from the divisions and attached to local territorial commands). A Gendarmerie platoon and a transport (Train) unit completed the divisional troops. The Field Army also had one Cavalry Division, consisting of 2 cavalry brigades (instead of the three planned in 1913). One brigade comprised the 1st and 2nd Guides and the other the 4th and 5th Lancers; the division had a group of horse artillery, and the single battalion of Carabinier-Cyclists. The Fortress branch included artillery and infantry regiments, modelled on the field regiments and divided between the fortified zones of Liège, Namur and Antwerp.

(In addition to the Belgian home army the kingdom also had colonial troops in central Africa, but unlike their British and French counterparts these were not committed to the war on the European continent. Details will be found in Men-at-Arms 379: *Armies in East Africa 1914–18*. The Belgian troops made a solid contribution to the campaigns against the German Cameroons and German East Africa, and after the Allied victory Belgium was awarded the former German colonies of Rwanda and Burundi under the terms of the Treaty of Versailles.)

The defence plan

Given the country's neutrality, the plans of the Belgian General Staff were obliged to assume that any one of the neighbouring nations might be a potential enemy. Since the national territory measured only about 150 miles east to west by 100 miles north to south, in case of invasion it was judged necessary to concentrate the main force behind rivers and in the three fortified zones to defend the country until support could arrive from the guarantors of Belgian neutrality. While the field army carried out a mobile defence the fortress garrisons were to remain in the supposed safety of their massive brick and concrete defences manning sunken steel artillery turrets.

The Citadel of Antwerp was the basis of the *'Réduit National'*. Between 1859 and 1870 a ring of 13 forts had been constructed around the city, followed by another 17 works still unfinished in 1914. In basing her hopes on this ultimate core of resistance, Belgium was not alone in over-estimating the military value of such defences; fortresses all over Europe had been rendered obsolete by the enormous recent progress in the design and production of heavy siege artillery. The most modern of the Belgian forts could not resist shells of calibres greater than 21cm, but they were going to find themselves facing Skoda 30.5cm and Krupp 42cm 'mortars' (super-heavy howitzers). The forts of Liège and Namur, covering bridges and roads in the Meuse valley as well as serving as bridgeheads for a counter-offensive, were all built in concrete after the designs of Gen Brialmont; but even after that brilliant engineer had obtained sufficient funds to augment their protection they were no more able than those at Antwerp to withstand a modern siege.

*   *   *

On 28 June 1914, in the streets of Sarajevo, a Bosnian Serb student assassinated the Archduke Franz Ferdinand, heir to the Austro-Hungarian throne. With German support, on 23 July Austria-Hungary sent an effectively unfulfillable ten-point ultimatum to the Serbian government, with the demand that it be accepted within 48 hours. In fact the Serbs agreed to all but one of these demands, but Austria-Hungary nonetheless broke off diplomatic relations on 25 July, and declared war three days later. The Russian government, which had pledged to uphold Serbian independence, mobilized its military reserves on 30 July. This resulted in Germany declaring war against Russia on 1 August and, two days later, against the latter's ally France.

Line infantrymen in the streets of Brussels. They wear their greatcoat skirts buttoned back as per regulations, and the large black leather ammunition pouch at the front of the belt. On campaign the shako pompons soon disappeared, and the oilcloth covers were often turned inside out – the highly reflective outer surface was too visible. (Langley Collection, Antwerp)

The German ultimatum

Under the terms of the Treaty of London upon which Belgian neutrality rested, the kingdom could not conclude any foreign alliance, even a defensive one. On the eve of the Franco-Prussian War in 1870 Great Britain, Prussia and France had signed a treaty with the intent of preserving Belgian neutrality in case of hostilities. Finally, in 1907, the 5th Hague Convention stipulated that the 'territory of neutral powers should be inviolable' and that belligerents were forbidden to send troops, munitions or supplies across that territory. Now, on the eve of World War I, Belgian neutrality was directly threatened.

On 2 August 1914 the German Ambassador, von Below, delivered a note to Belgian Foreign Minister Davignon. German troops were already occupying Luxemburg without resistance, and on the pretext that French forces intended to march on Germany across Belgian territory the note warned that in self-defence Germany was therefore obliged to send troops onto Belgian soil. If Belgium adopted a complaisant attitude towards this regrettably necessary violation of her neutrality, then Germany undertook to evacuate Belgian territory as soon as peace was concluded, and would pay for all requisitions necessary for her troops and compensation for all damage they might do. However, if Belgium acted in a hostile spirit, and especially if she raised obstacles by the active defence of her fortifications on the Meuse, then Germany would be obliged to regard Belgium as an enemy.

The Belgian government was given just 12 hours to reply to this infamous document. They replied that the intentions attributed to France had been expressly denied by the French government on 1 August. They referred to the Kingdom of Prussia's treaty obligations as a guarantor of Belgium's independence and neutrality, and declared that Belgium had always been faithful to her own undertakings as a neutral nation. The invasion with which the Germans were threatening Belgium would be an open violation of international law, and the German proposals could not be accepted without betraying both national honour and Belgium's treaty obligations to the other powers. Violation of her neutrality would be resisted with all the means in her power.

This reply by the government ensured Belgium's unassailable moral and legal position, and the German chancellor, Bethmann-Hollweg, cynically admitted as much (when informed by the British ambassador that Britain would go to war over violation of Belgian territory, he notoriously dismissed the treaty of neutrality as a mere 'scrap of paper'). Confident of triumph, he said in his speech to the Reichstag on 4 August 1914: 'The wrong that we are committing we shall repair as soon as our military aim has been achieved. To one who is

Men of the *Garde Civique* guarding harbour installations in Antwerp. This voluntary organization actually came under the Ministry of the Interior rather than the Ministry of War prior to mobilization. It was divided into three classes: the first, of all men between the ages of 21 and 32 not serving with the Army, who turned out for training ten times each year; the second, of men aged 33–50, only had to report their whereabouts three times a year. These classes both received uniforms; the third class, mainly of more elderly volunteers serving locally, had to make do with their civilian clothing. On 13 October 1914 the king disbanded the Civil Guard and the majority were absorbed as volunteers into the Army. (Langley Collection, Antwerp)

threatened as we are now, and who is struggling for his highest good, no other thought is permitted than trying to release himself. We are acting in self-defence, and necessity knows no law.'

That same day King Albert I of the Belgians informed Britain, France and Russia that the armed forces of Germany had that morning entered Belgian territory in violation of treaty obligations. His government was firmly determined to resist by all the means at their disposal, but he appealed to the three guaranteeing powers to co-operate in the defence of Belgian territory; the king's message ended with a declaration that Belgium would undertake to defend her fortified places. The next day Britain, France, and Russia promised their assistance. Britain's declaration of war against Germany on 4 August was officially the result not of her treaties with France and Russia, but of Germany's invasion of Belgium, whose independence Britain had guaranteed. British public sentiment was supportive of 'plucky little Belgium', and would become even more so over the coming weeks as reports of German conduct in occupied territory reached the outside world.

INVASION

If she hoped to win a war on two fronts Germany needed a swift victory over France while primitive Russia was still mobilizing her armies in the East. Although modified and weakened by the chief of the German General Staff, Gen von Moltke, the 'Schlieffen Plan' still envisaged holding-actions further south to draw the bulk of the French armies into battle in Alsace-Lorraine, while strong German armies on the right flank raced through neutral Belgium into northern France to hook around Paris from the north. In its modified form the plan involved 26 infantry and 5 cavalry divisions of the German First and Second Armies passing between Antwerp and Namur, pushing through Luxemburg and Belgium

Engineers (Génie) relaxing near Antwerp, August 1914. Note that they wear French-style képis but with fold-down flaps; this Engineer field cap would be the inspiration for the widely worn 'Yser cap' of winter 1914–15. (Royal Army Museum (RMA), Brussels)

and sweeping around the French fortified system to encircle the mass of her armies before Britain – should she declare war – would have time to intervene. Von Kluck's and von Bülow's armies had to cross Belgium fast, crushing her army with a maximum of violence if it offered the slightest resistance.

When Germany's intentions became clear, Belgium's only possible strategy was to attempt a delaying defence until the guaranteeing powers sent troops to her aid. The Belgian Field Army would be divided to resist the enemy's westwards and southwards thrusts. On the right wing the 3rd and 4th Army Divisions would concentrate around the fortified zones of Liège and Namur along the Meuse; meanwhile the other four divisions would concentrate on the left, further north between the rivers Gette and Dyle, within the square of territory Leuven-Tienen-Wavre-Perwez, in order to cover Brussels in the centre and Antwerp further north. The Belgian campaign of summer–autumn 1914 can be considered in four main phases: the defence of the fortified position of Liège, the defence of the line of the Gette and of the Namur zone, the defence of Antwerp, and the battle of the Yser.

The defence of Liège, August 1914

A few hours after the delivery of the reply to the German ultimatum the forces that had been massed on the frontier entered Belgium. During the morning of 4 August two cavalry divisions outflanked the fortified position of Liège on the north and arrived at Visé on the Meuse, but, finding the bridge broken and the passage guarded they withdrew towards their principal force, which was already standing before the advanced defences of the fortified city. General von Emmich had about 130,000 men and plentiful artillery; he expected that, faced with such a disproportionate force, Gen Leman would capitulate rather than make a useless attempt to defend Liège. When a German demand that Leman give passage to the Germans was rejected Emmich immediately proceeded to attack the forts of Chaudfontaine, Fléron, Evegnée, Barchon and Pontisse. Nine brigades stormed across the fields in between the different forts, but were everywhere repulsed with such heavy losses that several divisions were withdrawn into Germany; this spread such a panic that at Aachen (Aix-la-Chapelle) librarians started removing archives for safety.

The invasion of tiny, neutral Belgium caused an outburst in the international press, soon followed by a chorus of admiration for the Belgians' unexpectedly stubborn resistance against the overwhelming strength of the German armies. Every day the Belgians held back the German advance was another day gained for the Allies to prepare their own defence. (*War Illustrated*, Brussels; Langley Collection, Antwerp)

9

Lieutenant-General Gérard Mathieu Leman, born in Liège on 8 January 1851, was responsible for the king's military education before the war. Commandant of the Military School in Brussels (1905) and member of the National Defence Committee (1913), he would take overall command of the forts surrounding Liège, and during the initial stages of the battle the Germans were unable to break through. They had to take the time to bring up super-heavy artillery and bombard the forts one by one until they succeeded in knocking them out. Leman was knocked unconscious and buried in the debris of Fort de Loncin when its magazine exploded with catastrophic effects on 15 August, killing some 250 of the garrison; he was rescued by German troops. A prisoner of war in Germany until 1917, when he was released on health grounds, Leman insisted that the report of his capture mention that he did not surrender but was taken prisoner while unconscious. After the war he returned home to a hero's welcome and ennoblement as a count, and died on 17 October 1920. Leman's defence of Liège had delayed the German advance for three priceless days. See also Plate A1. (Nelsons; Langley Collection, Antwerp)

German reinforcements were brought up in large numbers, and started an outflanking movement that threatened with encirclement the Belgian troops holding the intervals between the forts. These field units were compelled to withdraw; however, the forts themselves held out, the last only capitulating on 16 and 17 August after Forts Chaudfontaine and de Loncin had been destroyed with heavy loss of life by monstrous explosions when German shells penetrated the magazines. The German casualties outside Liège have been estimated at 42,712 men, but much more serious was the loss of precious time. The unexpected check suffered by the vanguard held up the invading army in enormous traffic jams; the overcrowding of roads and railways caused such confusion inside Germany that the whole army had to mark time for several days, which enabled the French Army to carry out its mobilization and concentration.

Even though their garrisons were doomed, the time it was costing the invaders to put the outdated fortresses out of action would have a real influence on the outcome of the 1914 campaign.

The defence of the Gette and Namur, August 1914

While Gen von Emmich's X Corps was held up before Liège the main Belgian Field Army took up positions on the river Gette, a natural line of defence about 20 miles behind the Meuse. It remained in observation until 18 August, fighting several successful actions against the invaders; one of these, at Haelen in the province of Limburg on 12 August, became known as 'the Battle of the Silver Helmets'. Here the Belgian Cavalry Division, including the Carbinier-Cyclist Battalion, inflicted heavy casualties on four of the six regiments of the

A revolving cupola at Fort de Fléron, Liège, mounting twin 21cm guns. The German bombardment from 9 August had destroyed all but one of the cupolas by the time the fort garrison capitulated on the 14th. (RMA, Brussels)

A German 42cm 'mortar' – actually a super-heavy howitzer – as used against the Liège forts. They were less precise than the 30.5cm Skoda and 21cm pieces, but the impact of their one-ton shells was more devastating. General Leman described the experience: 'We heard them coming. We heard them howling through the air, and finally the noise of a furious hurricane, which ended with a terrific thunderclap, and then gigantic clouds of dust and smoke rose above the trembling ground.' Note the 'caterpillar tracks' attached to prevent the wheels sinking into the ground. (Nelsons; Langley Collection, Antwerp)

German cavalry corps commanded by Gen von der Marwitz, driving them back in disorder and remaining masters of the field. The German attempt to cut off the main Field Army from Antwerp was checked, and this action proved that cavalry charges alone would never again be able to secure a decision when facing repeating firearms.

Despite such creditable episodes, however, the whole countryside around Liège fell to the overwhelming numbers of the invaders. More than 11 German army corps were facing Belgium's handful of divisions; even excluding those corps that were moving towards France across the provinces of Luxemburg and Namur, about 500,000 German troops naturally quite ignorant of the complexities and difficulties attending the concentration of modern armies, were impatiently waiting for visible help from the French high command. In the south the French Fifth Army had a corps holding the bridges over the Sambre between Floreffe and Tamines; three more corps arrived in the neighbourhood of Philippeville on 19 August, but they were threatened by three German corps extending from Yvoir to Beauraing. In the meantime, the small British Expeditionary Force (BEF) had landed in France and was marching to the south of the Sambre towards Maubeuge; it was therefore impossible for the Allied armies to link up inside Belgium. The Belgian Field Army, with a total strength of about two corps, remained alone and in close confrontation with forces of more than four times its strength. Assailed on its front and flanks, it was in imminent danger of being cut off from its indispensable rear supply base at Antwerp and, had it held its positions, the outcome on 19 August could not be doubted. Accordingly, on the afternoon of the 18th, King Albert ordered a retreat towards the north-west.

Brussels capitulated on 20 August, and on the same day two German corps under Gen von Gallwitz opened the siege of Namur, isolated by the Belgian retreat. The 4th Army Division, which had been defending the approaches to the city, was forced on 23 August to begin an extremely difficult retreat through the woods between the Sambre and Meuse; it managed to reach France, and from thence it was sent back to Antwerp. As at the forts of Liège, the very first salvoes from the four batteries of German 30.5cm and 42cm artillery destroyed the steel cupolas of the Namur forts, and thereafter the garrisons suffered days of merciless pounding as the heavy artillery dealt with them methodically in twos and threes. The last, Forts de Suarlée and d'Émines, fell on 24 August.

The Germans bypassed Antwerp, which remained a threat to their right flank, and swept on through Belgium, causing great suffering to the civilian population. After marching through Belgium, Luxemburg and the Ardennes the Germans advanced, in the latter half of August, into northern France; there they met both the French under Gen Joffre, and the initial six divisions of the BEF under Gen Sir John French. A series of engagements known as the Battle of the Frontiers ensued; key phases included the battles of Charleroi and Mons. A general Allied retreat followed, punctuated by actions such as the battle of Le Cateau, the siege of Maubeuge and the battle of St Quentin.

The defence of Antwerp, August–October 1914

Once the line of the Gette was forced the German armies occupied the country methodically. By 20 August they were in Brussels, where, though crushed with requisitions, the people of the capital accepted their fate calmly. In the rest of the country the Germans immediately instituted a regime of 'frightfulness'; cities like Louvain, Visé, Dinant and Aarschot were burned down, while large numbers of civilians, including women and priests, were summarily shot. The Germans alleged that these victims had been in areas from which their troops had been fired upon after the withdrawal of Belgian soldiers, but their citing of the precedent of the French *francs-tireurs* of 1870–71 as justification for their shooting of hostages was dishonest; the frustrated German high command was probably intent on forcing Belgium into a premature and separate peace by terrorizing her population. (The war crimes committed by the German Army during this period became known as the 'Rape of Belgium'; after the Great War some people came to believe that the horror stories were largely Allied propaganda, but in more recent years many of the atrocities have been confirmed and fully documented.) Together with her initial disdain for international treaties, this wanton destruction and ill-treatment forfeited Germany's honour in the eyes of the world from the very first weeks of the war, condemning her troops to be known as 'Huns'.

Having retreated to Antwerp, the 'national refuge', the Belgian Army finally seemed to have been knocked out of the struggle. Three days after taking Brussels, Gen von Gallwitz's corps pushed the Belgian 4th Army

Division to the west and started the encirclement of the port and its fortifications. The Germans resumed their rush towards Paris, leaving only a few corps of the Landwehr before Antwerp, from which they believed they had nothing to fear, but in the event the Belgian Army did not confine itself to a passive defence. In order to support the Allied effort at the Marne and to menace enemy lines of communication the Belgians executed two sallies from Antwerp, on 23 August and 7 September 1914. Losses were severe, but these sorties held back in Belgium three German divisions that were on their way to France in order to reinforce von Kluck's First Army, then in retreat from the Marne to the Aisne. The anxiety caused to the Germans by this evidence of Belgian offensive spirit was so keen that as soon as they had settled their front to the north of the Aisne they decided to lay siege to the fortress city and finally rid themselves of an opponent whom they affected to scorn but who nonetheless was causing them serious disquiet.

On 28 September the Germans, having brought up their heavy artillery, began an intense bombardment of the outer defences. Shells slammed into Forts Waelhem and Wavre Ste Catherine; at the latter – as at the Liège forts – a shell penetrated the ammunition magazine, whose explosion reduced part of the fort to rubble. Another shell fell directly into the Antwerp waterworks located just behind the fort, cutting the water supply to the city. The concrete of the fort roofs simply dissolved under the continued explosive impacts, and the lack of adequate ventilation or sanitary facilities drove the defenders out as the dust and fumes became intolerable. The fate of the fortress was sealed, since its communications with the Allies were difficult and the garrisons were too weak to build improvised trenches and works to replace those that were destroyed. British reinforcements came too late and too few in number to make any serious difference. The hopes based on the *Réduit*

From the first days of the war Belgian armoured motorcars mounting machine guns and light artillery pieces proved their worth, both in making up for Belgium's relative lack of reconnaissance aircraft and in covering the Army's retreats; those based in the fortified zones would go out every morning to locate the latest German positions. Mainly constructed in the Minerva factory in Antwerp, they were a popular subject for foreign press photographers. (Langley Collection, Antwerp; & *Fighting in Flanders*)

National were vain; nevertheless, aware of the painful moral effect that the fall of Antwerp would produce, the Belgian high command organized a stubborn resistance while preparing for the Field Army's retreat.

The evacuation of Antwerp was an extremely demanding operation, as the whole base of the Belgian defence had to be transferred westward. Ostend was selected as the new centre of resistance, and the wounded, prisoners, supplies of all kinds, the unit depots and the untrained recruits of the new levy were all withdrawn. The Army thus gained freedom of action within Antwerp and outside, and could leave the fortress as soon as the city was judged to be irretrievably compromised. The defence – in which the British Royal Naval Brigade bore a brave part – continued until 7 October. On that day all the exterior lines of the fortress were cut, while a powerful German army was threatening Ghent and Flanders. Retreat was still possible but became more problematic with every passing hour, since the Army could now reach the sea coast only through an exceedingly narrow passage along the Dutch frontier offering very few roads and one single-track railway.

The retreat was carried out in good order and very rapidly, beginning on the night of 6 October, and on the morning of the 7th the whole army crossed to the left bank of the Scheldt. German forces had also crossed the river, however, and were sighted upstream at the gates of Ghent. This was one of the tragic hours of the war; at one time the Army was in danger of being encircled, cut off from its allies and thrown back into neutral Holland (where large elements did indeed have to take refuge). Fortunately, Franco-British reinforcements arrived in time. The French naval brigade of *fusiliers-marins* under command of Adm Ronarc'h, and part of the British 7th Division, landed in Ghent and took up positions outside that town, where they pressed the Germans back with the support of two groups of Belgian artillery. This resistance gained valuable hours, and while the Belgian gunners, French sailors and British infantrymen covered their retreat the Field Army quickly moved towards Ostend. On 10 October the last fort of Antwerp capitulated, and on the 15th what was left of the Belgian Field Army and the French naval infantry took up their positions on the river Yser.

THE BATTLE OF THE YSER, 1914

The German defeat at the First Battle of the Marne would herald the beginnings of a static front in the West that was to last for the next three years. Now, the opposing forces tried to outflank each other to the north in the 'Race for the Sea'.

On the morning of the surrender of Antwerp nearly the whole of the remaining Belgian Army stood massed behind the canal leading from Ghent to Terneuzen. However, the French left was fighting in the neighbourhood of Arras, and the BEF, marching up from the Aisne, was forming in the neighbourhood of St Omer. Under these conditions, if the Belgians had made a stand they might have been driven to the Dutch frontier and to the sea by the greatly superior German forces in Belgium. After consultation with the French and British staffs, the Belgian high command decided to retire as far as the Yser. This line would offer many advantages, since it was the prolongation of the Franco-British front that ran from Lassigny south towards Arras; the Belgian Army would stand between the English Channel, where British warships were cruising, and the Allies to the south. Finally, the character of the countryside lent itself to the defensive.

The terrain of the Yser is a vast flat plain, covered with rich meadows and fertile fields and bare of any features; by mid-October it was 'a boundless, flat, green surface [with] the patches of land and pastures divided by moats full of water'. This landscape rendered infantry action difficult, especially as the roads were few and poor. The Yser, which runs straight to the sea from Diksmuide to Nieuport, is not much more than 20 yards wide, but in terrain of this character it nonetheless offered a perfectly defensible line – the more so as close behind it lies the railway embankment between Diksmuide and Nieuport, forming a kind of supporting rampart. On the other hand, the country is so waterlogged that it is nearly impossible to dig trenches or build underground shelters.

On 15 October 1914 the Belgian Field Army took up its positions on the Yser, where the remnants were reorganized. They had suffered 9,000 killed, 15,000 wounded, and several tens of thousands captured, missing, or forced across the Dutch border into internment. The total available manpower had thus been reduced to at most 80,000 men, but of these only about 48,000 still carried rifles, supported by 184 machine guns and 306 artillery pieces. They were tired out by a long, hard retreat, and the high command feared that those still in the ranks would be completely demoralized by the surrender of Antwerp and the German occupation of much of the country. But a royal proclamation told the men that they must hold, that the safety of all depended on their courage and steadfastness; they listened, and they did hold.

The fort of Waelhem, one of those defending the *Réduit National* of Antwerp. Built in 1891, it was modernized to resist 21cm guns in 1911. After five days of bombardment by 28cm, 30.5cm and 42cm artillery, starting on 28 September, the commandant was obliged to capitulate on 2 October after the destruction of the last intact cupola. (*La Belgique et la Guerre*, Vol 3; Brussels, 1926)

On Wednesday, 7 October, after the outer forts of Antwerp had been silenced, the Belgian government was transferred to Ostend; this photo shows the removal of books and papers from Antwerp. Subsequently, when Ostend became untenable, the government was provisionally established at Le Havre, France. (Langley Collection, Antwerp)

Retreat to the river Yser, early October 1914; a *Times* correspondent reported: 'Under cover of the night the last division of the Belgian Army filed out of Antwerp unmolested by the enemy, and since the early hours of the morning till late evening I have seen repeated the singularly impressive scenes of yesterday – men, and still more men, horses, wagons, big guns, small guns, howitzers, captured German [field] kitchens, motorcars, omnibuses, and all the wonderful paraphernalia of modern warfare. Some batteries were without guns, which had been lost or put out of action.' The fall of Antwerp would cost the Belgian Army some 60,000 men captured by the Germans or interned in neutral Holland, but the survivors' success in plugging the Yser gap was of the highest importance to supporting the French and British armies during the 'Race to the Sea'. (Langley Collection, Antwerp)

At that time the front of the French Tenth Army was strongly organized up as far as La Bassée, but from there to the Channel coast all that stood in the way of the German 'Race for the Sea' was the Belgian Army, Adm Ronarc'h's French naval brigade, the British 7th Infantry and 3rd Cavalry divisions, and the 87th and 89th divisions of French Territorials. Later in the battle these formations would be reinforced by a French cavalry corps of four divisions and the 42nd Infantry Division. The Germans made a series of attacks on the Belgian formations, which they considered the weakest element on the Yser line, in order to outflank the Franco-British left wing. Hence the importance of the part played by the Belgian Army and the French naval brigade; by holding their positions – alone from 15 to 23 October, then with the reinforcement of the French 42nd Division until 10 November – these already tired soldiers secured Allied success in the first battle of Flanders.

As early as 16 October a German probe was repulsed fairly easily at Diksmuide, but the pressure quickly built up. The next day German artillery started shelling the whole front; on the 18th the bridgehead of Mannekensvere outside Nieuport was carried by a violent infantry attack, as were most of the advanced posts on the right bank of the Yser, despite gunfire support from Royal Navy shallow-draught monitors. On the 19th the last pockets held by the Belgians east of the river were lost, and the French sailors were called back to the left bank. On 20 October Lombaertzyde was lost, but Diksmuide, although attacked with great vigour, still resisted; the *fusiliers-marins* and Belgian 11th and

12th Line regiments held their positions under violent bombardment, followed by repeated infantry attacks carried out by deep masses that were constantly renewed.

The German Fourth Army now had seven divisions facing the Belgians and the French sailors, and it became urgent to define the defensive front. The Allied high command decided that the Belgian Army's sector would stop at St Jacques Capelle, a little south of Diksmuide (see map, p20), giving them a front of 20km (12½ miles). The French Territorials would occupy the space between St Jacques and Ypres, and Ypres would be covered by Gen Rawlinson's two British divisions to the east.

A Belgian general (right) and his aides. The officer on the left, wearing goggles, probably drives a motorcycle or motorcar. The man in the centre wears the officers' single-breasted M1913 tunic with sleeve ranking. (Langley Collection, Antwerp)

20–25 October

During the night of 20/21 October the Germans delivered an extremely violent bombardment, which extended to the second lines so as to prevent the arrival of reserves. During the afternoon of the 21st infantry attacks were launched on the sector Nieuport-Diksmuide and on Diksmuide itself. Trenches were taken and retaken, and all the Belgian reserves were committed; the artillery did great execution among the attackers, but the Germans maintained their pressure. An attempt on the river line at Schoorbakke was driven back by the 4th Line Regt, but by dawn on the 22nd the attackers had crossed the river at Tervaete, and this bridgehead was maintained against all Belgian counter-attacks. The moat of the Yser had been crossed and the defenders were at the end of their endurance; at one point no relief could get forward and men who had spent 72 hours in the trenches had to be ordered to hold on. On 15 October the Belgian high command had been asked to withstand the German onslaught on the Yser for 24 hours; in the end they had to wait eight days for Allied reinforcements.

Belgian counter-attacks north of Nieuport reached Lombaertzyde and Bamburgh Farm on the right bank, and at last, on 23 October, the French 42nd Division (Gen Grosseti) arrived at Nieuport to join the line. Feeling that resistance was growing weaker in the Diksmuide sector, the Germans redoubled their attacks there. They now gained a bridgehead at Schoorbakke, further threatening the defenders of what was now a salient. At dawn on the 24th three German assaulting columns, each about 7,000 strong, marched upon the trenches at Tervaete in close formation and, in spite of suffering heavy losses, succeeded in taking the Belgian front line along a dyke. A battalion of Belgian Grenadiers commanded by Maj Henri d'Oultremont and two battalions of French sailors delivered a desperate counter-attack; they reached the dyke, but were unable to hold it, and Maj d'Oultremont and Capt van Leathem were among the many killed. The Germans had gained a solid footing in the front-line trenches along the left riverbank, and Tervaete was occupied; some wavering Belgian troops left the shattered trenches to force their way back through the cordon of military police.

French naval infantry – *fusiliers-marins* – of the brigade commanded by Admiral Ronarc'h, one of the first Allied formations to support the Belgian Army during the invasion and a mainstay of the defence of the Yser line in autumn 1914. (Langley Collection, Antwerp)

The situation was highly critical, with both Diksmuide and Nieuport in danger of being outflanked by river crossings. With all haste, Col Meiser despatched 1st Bn/11th Line Regt to the threatened point; led by Maj Descamps, they managed to hold back the German rush for long enough to buy time for four other Belgian battalions and the naval brigade's reserve to come up. Colonel Jacques took his faltering units back into the fight: 'No, boys – not that way, always straight ahead!'. By the end of that terrible day a solid second line had been established along a canal called the Beverdijk, but the staff were receiving reports that the troops were worn out and that their morale was such that any incident might cause panic.

Diksmuide had been attacked no less fiercely than Tervaete, and an incident that occurred during the night showed how precarious the situation remained. The attack on the trenches had by then slackened off, with only occasional shots still being fired. Suddenly, in the dark of the night, a troop of some hundreds of Germans led by a major, and probably guided by a spy, appeared in Diksmuide town square. Nobody knew how they had forced the lines, but they were driving about 20 Belgian prisoners before them with rifle-butts. Amid confused shouts of 'The Boches! the Boches!', the Germans ran all the way to the bridge over the Yser, no one knowing whether they were fugitives or enemies; at last, when there could no longer be any mistake, a machine gun placed near the bridge began to fire into the crowd. About 30 Germans fell, and others fled back into Diksmuide and took shelter in cellars, where Belgian troops would find them at daybreak. The German major led the rest of his raiders on under cover of darkness towards Caeskerke. At a French naval brigade first aid station – fully lighted – a volley of rifle shots struck down surgeon Duguet and Abbé Le Helloco, chaplain of the 2nd Regiment. The raiders were then checked by a gate that had been closed in time, and sailors hurried up from their nearby trenches. Under their fire the Germans scattered over the neighbouring meadows, and threatened their prisoners with death if they did not direct them towards the artillery batteries; no one spoke, and the Germans shot them down, Cdr Jeanniot of the *fusiliers-marins* dying at the hand of the German major. At break of day the Germans who were left were surrounded in batches; several fell under the bayonets of the infuriated soldiers, and four were convicted of murder and executed by the French admiral's orders.

On 25 October the German advance ran out of steam and stopped just in time. The Belgian Army could do no more; its overworked artillery batteries had many unserviceable guns and those that were left were down to 100 rounds apiece. The Belgian high command then took the decision to withdraw the line slightly to the railway embankment, and to protect that line with an obstacle that could not be passed: an inundation.

Opening the sluices

Deliberate flooding was a classic defensive tactic in Flanders. These lowlands were reclaimed from the sea and the marshes, and are managed by a system of drainage and irrigation that dates back to the Middle Ages. To flood the ground covered by the German front lines it would be sufficient to open the sluices in Nieuport that gave access to the Beverdijk, and to close them again before the ebb tide. The system of canals and manually-operated sluice gates was complex, and the exact results depended upon the tides and winds. However, under the direction of one Louis Kogge, who had been in charge of the Beverdijk sluices for many years, all necessary measures were taken, and from 27 October seawater began to mix with that of the canals. The flood oozed up on all sides to suck down German guns, fill the trenches, and imprison in their strongpoints those defenders imprudently left in them by the German command (these isolated garrisons either surrendered one by one, or were drowned while trying to escape). Gradually the whole front between Nieuport and Dixmuide was covered, from the Yser westwards to the railway embankment.

This unexpected ally of the Entente seemed to surprise the Germans, and on the 27th and 28th their activity slackened along the whole Yser front, but on 29 October they recovered and launched attacks in depth on the French 42nd Division. The village of Pervijse, slightly west of the railway line opposite Tervaete, was heavily shelled and for a short time was seriously threatened by infantry attacks. In the ruins Gen Grosetti ordered an armchair to be brought and sat calmly in it for three hours, directing the battle: 'Now, boys, at my time of life one cannot run. You aren't going to leave me in the hands of the Boches, are you?' The Germans launched fifteen waves of attack upon the trenches at Pervijse, but the village was still holding out when they finally tired of the attempt. On 30 October the German efforts were directed towards Ramscapelle to the north of Pervijse. For a short time the line was broken and the village occupied, but the enemy was allowed no time to consolidate before a Belgian Line regiment and one of Zouaves delivered a counter-attack that cleared the village and retook the lost trenches.

This proved to be the last gasp of the German offensive on the Yser, which was now finally balked. During eight days some 48,000 men of the Belgian Army and 8,000 French infantry had held back seven German divisions with a formidable artillery. The Belgian Army had lost a quarter of its effectives and an even higher proportion of its junior leaders (for instance, the 11th Line had lost 17 officers out of 44, and the 12th Line 19 out of 42). The French brigade of *fusiliers-marins* had been still more cruelly tried; they had lost half their numbers, and of the 24 naval

Flooding the desired area in a controlled manner was a complex task, and to keep Belgian positions from flooding engineers had to build a sandbag dam at the viaduct of Koolhof, where a siphon would normally allow seawater to flow under the Veurne (Furnes) Canal. In October 1915 this barrier would be rebuilt in concrete. (*Nieuport 1914–1918*; Paris, Liège & London, 1922)

As a result of the flooding, large areas of Flanders disappeared under a sheet of seawater. Most of the farms and villages in the region were built on the higher ground, which allowed both the Allies and the Germans to use these islets as observation and sniper posts; on the Belgian side most of them were linked by means of precarious wooden walkways. (Author's collection)

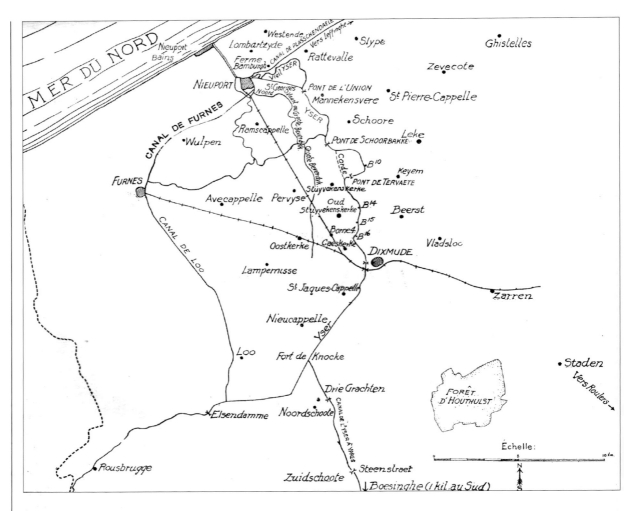

The following place names and labels appear on the map:

MER DU NORD

Nieuport Bains · Westende · SCHENDAELE · Vers leffinghe · Slype · Ghistelles

Lombartzyde · CANAL DE PLASSCHENDAELE · Rattevalle · Zevecote

Ferme Bamburgh · VIR YSER

NIEUPORT · St Georges Noord · PONT DE L'UNION · Mannekensvere · St Pierre-Cappelle

CANAL DE FURNES · Ramscappelle · Schoore · Leke

Wulpen · PONT DE SCHOORBAKKE

FURNES · B10 · Keyem · PONT DE TERVAETE

Avecappelle · Pervyse · Stuyvekenskerke · B14 · Beerst

Oud Stuyvekenskerke · B15 · B16

Barne4 · Caeskerke · Vladsloo

Oostkerke · DIXMUDE

Lampernisse

CANAL DE LOO · St Jaques-Cappelle · Zarren

Nieucappelle · Yser

Loo · Fort de Knocke · Staden · Vers Roulers

Drie Grachten · FORÊT D'HOUTHULST

Elsendamme · Noordschoote · CANAL DE L'YSER À YPRES

Echelle:

Rousbrugge · Zuidschoote · Steenstraet · Boesinghe (1 kil. au Sud)

lieutenants commanding their companies 22 had been killed. But in the end the road to Calais had been closed against the Germans on that flank; now they would try to reach it by another path – as the Battle of the Yser ended, the First Battle of Ypres began. There the ordeal of the BEF was to last until the middle of November, by which time the old Flemish city had been shelled into a mere pile of rubble. The steadfastness of the British and French troops defending that sector would break the German offensive as it had been broken on the Yser, where the Belgians and the French sailors had put up the resistance that allowed the Allies to win their second victory and to stop the invaders' march.

The Yser front, 1915–18. The railway line slanting south-east in a straight line from Nieuport on the coast to Dixmude marks the actual Belgian front line after the flooding of the Yser river flats to the east of it. St Jacques Cappelle immediately south of Dixmude marks the Belgian right flank. The Ypres Salient is just off the map, south of the Houthulst Forest.

REBUILDING THE ARMY

After the supreme effort on the Yser, by troops who had already been cruelly tested for two and a half months, the roll call and the inventory showed that a new Belgian Army would have to be created if it was to take any further active part in the war.

In August the Field Army had numbered some 120,000 men, in addition to about 100,000 in the fortress garrisons and the Civil Guard

Belgian soldiers on their way to the Flanders trenches. Persistent rain turned the whole district into a quagmire; many of the roads were knee-deep in mud, and baulks of timber had to be laid down before they could be used. The column shown here is provided with spades and picks for work on the roads. Note the ruined farmhouses in the background; many Flemish homes and small villages were literally obliterated by bombardment, while others were reduced to bare walls gaping with holes. (Langley Collection, Antwerp)

July 1916: this squad training to crawl towards barbed wire under fire while piling sandbags ahead of them can be seen under magnification to wear the khaki uniform and the soft-crowned British-style service cap. In Flemish, sandbags were (and still are) called *Vaderlandertjes* – 'little patriots'. (*N'oublions jamais*, Brussels, 1919; Service Photographique de l'Armée Belge)

together. Large numbers had been lost in the battles around Liège and Namur and during the siege of Antwerp, and part of the garrison of that city had been compelled to cross the frontier into Holland, where about 30,000 men had been interned. In the surrenders of Liège and Antwerp the Germans had taken about 30,000 prisoners; finally, on the Yser, the Belgian army had lost at least 12,000 more. Those that were left were exhausted, their uniforms in tatters, many of them barefoot, and the older age classes were in such a poor physical state that they temporarily had to be taken to the rear.

The first need was for new recruits, but with the greater part of Belgium now occupied by the Germans these had to be sought among the refugees who had followed the army ahead of the invaders. The government trusted to their patriotism, and when it issued a call for voluntary enlistment its hopes were greatly exceeded. Not only did the refugees answer the king's appeal in large numbers, so also did young men from the occupied districts. Although the lines were closely guarded, and the Germans decreed severe penalties not only for men who tried to cross but also for their families, several thousand young Belgians escaped to Holland and even to England to put themselves at the disposal of the government, now based at Le Havre. This voluntary response enabled the reconstitution as early as 1915 of an army of six infantry and two cavalry divisions. Subsequently, a conscription decree of 21 July 1916 called to arms all Belgian men between 18 and 40 years of age living in neutral or Allied countries. These new levies provided the reserves necessary to hold the defensive front for which Belgium took responsibility, and for the future offensives in which she was determined to take a share proportionate to her forces.

Many of the regular officers who had been engaged in the 1914 campaigns had been killed, wounded or captured. The character of the army had also undergone a change, so that the command structure had to be rejuvenated and filled with a new spirit. The problems of providing cadres for rapidly expanding wartime armies were shared by all the combatant nations, but were particularly acute for a small country like Belgium. Even at the outbreak of war she had had only some 3,200 of the 5,500 officers needed on mobilization, and had had to resort to emergency measures such as commissioning and promoting the pupils of the Military School and Staff College and recalling retired officers to the colours. After the battle of the Yser a complete reorganization was gradually put in place. A series of training schools were opened in France; the infantry had

Throughout the war in Flanders an essential task of the Belgian Army was to control the water level of the flooded areas. Here Belgian engineers have built a dam on the Yser river lock near Nieuport in 1917. (*Nieuport 1914–1918*)

a centre in Gaillon, and the artillery settled first at Audresselles before transferring to Onival. Among the young engineers who enlisted many were suitable for officer training, and these maintained the Europe-wide reputation enjoyed by the Belgian technical branches. Large numbers of engineer officers were recruited from among the refugees in France and England, and former sergeants in the regular army were also promoted; all of these rose to the considerable challenge of creating model defences across the waterlogged plain of the Yser.

During the October fighting the Belgian artillery had been so overworked that it was practically worn out. At the outbreak of the war it had been undergoing a complete reorganization; the siege guns ordered from Krupp had not been delivered, and though the field artillery was excellent in quality its numbers were insufficient. In 1914 the endurance, technical skill and initiative of the officers had to some extent compensated for the shortage of guns, but in 1915 the branch had to be rebuilt almost from scratch. Half the guns were out of commission – as were many of the infantry's rifles and machine guns. Everything that could still be of some service had to be repaired urgently, and new arms and ammunition had to be procured in quantity. From October 1914 repair workshops were improvised in Calais for artillery pieces, rifles, motorcars, military wagons and harness. German stores captured by the French and British armies were put at Belgium's disposal and overhauled. At Le Havre an abandoned factory was transformed into a production line for shells; its first task was to adapt ammunition for the French 75mm gun for use in the Krupp design of the same calibre used by the Belgian Army (this soon proved an unsuccessful expedient). Belgium purchased rifles, machine guns and artillery to make up the shortfalls, and in the spring of 1915 the army – which had not for a moment left the Yser front – was ready for battle again, taking a creditable part in the heavy fighting that occurred at Steenstraete and Lizerne in April and May.

In August 1915 the Minister of War decided to build the necessary ordnance factories in the neighbourhood of Le Havre, leaving only the repair workshops at Calais. At the same time a mill for the production of explosives and a small-arms factory for the supply of rifles and carbines were established in England. Soon the Belgian Army possessed 75 times more wireless telegraphy sets than it had at the beginning of the war, and 400 times more searchlights; it acquired nearly 16,000 motorcycles and bicycles, established a complete plant for airships, and gathered a particularly bold, devoted and active corps of airmen.

* * *

By spring 1917 the army comprised six Army Divisions and two Cavalry Divisions; non-divisional units included two heavy artillery regiments totalling 21 batteries, a railway battalion, and units of other supporting arms. The composition of the divisions was as follows:

1st Army Division: 3 infantry brigades, 1 artillery brigade, 1 Lancer regiment, 2 engineer battalions, a divisional cyclist company, a transport unit and a rehabilitation company.
2nd, 5th & 6th Army Divisions: each as 1st Div, but minus cavalry regiment.
3rd & 4th Army Divisions: each as 1st Div, but 2 Lancer squadrons only.
1st & 2nd Cavalry Divisions: each 2 cavalry brigades, 1 Carabinier-Cyclist battalion, 1 horse artillery group, 1 company *pontonnier-pionniers cyclistes,* and a transport unit.

THE WATCH ON THE YSER, 1915–17

At the end of the battle of the Yser the Belgian Army held such an extended front that from the beginning of 1915 to the middle of 1917 not one of its divisions could be wholly relieved, since it commanded no strategic reserve. (When possible, of course, units were briefly rotated into the rear areas, where the usual belt of logistics and communications, billets and aid stations paralleled the front line and offered some notional safety from the more routine bombardments.) The character of the soil on this front also rendered its task particularly exhausting, unhealthy and difficult. As Roland de Marès wrote in the *Temps,* the Belgian soldiers' main enemy at the front was not the Germans, it was water – water slowly undermining and destroying the most solid works, invading the trenches and filling the saps. The winter of 1914–15 was hideously trying. In order to provide the indispensable minimum of comfort to the soldiers during their endless ordeal in the mud, everything had to be made out of nothing. After a tour of the front, de Marès would write:

I had inspected the trenches and battlefields of the Yser in November 1914. I had wandered through the smoking ruins of villages in all their fresh horror; I had seen the shattered walls of the Cloth Hall of Ypres ruddy in the tragic evening light; I had looked upon German corpses floating on the muddy waters of the inundation. Now, after two years, I have passed through the same desolate spots again; their desolation has perhaps become still more painful, because it has assumed the appearance of something habitual. Ramscapelle, Pervijse, Lampernisse, Nieuwcapelle, Reninghe, Boesinghe – those villages then were heaps of bleeding ruins, but they were still alive with warlike sounds. Algerian sharpshooters were quartered in the schoolhouse of Reninghe, which had escaped the bombardment by a miracle, and they were filling it with cheerful noise. Belgian soldiers in tattered uniforms followed the drenched roads, passing relieving columns of French Territorials, Zouaves and sailors. The

Unlike the Allies along most of the Western Front the Belgian Army could not dig trenches below ground level in the 'Water Sector', since the water table was less than 2ft below the surface. This shows embanked Belgian defences behind a flooded area, with the drainage channels needed to keep the worst of the water out of the shelters. (Author's collection)

posts of the several nations that had taken part in the battle were in close, neighbourly touch. At Furnes, at Loo and in other villages and townships immediately behind the front there was a picturesque mingling of all the uniforms of the Allied armies, and under the unceasing thumping of shells the vast grey plain seemed to be teeming with troops and transport. The battle was just over, perhaps soon to begin again.

In 1916, when I revisited the Belgian front, the cannon were still roaring in broken squalls, but over a desert. The Belgian Army was holding the Yser front alone, but, obeying the necessities of trench war, it was in hiding; it was present everywhere, but nowhere to be seen. For kilometres our motorcar meandered along empty roads, passing through the sites of villages where the ruins had, after two years, clad themselves with branches and weeds. When we stopped for a moment an officer or soldier would emerge from the rubbish heaps, leaving his shelter, his trench or his guardpost to see who had come to break the deadly monotony of his heroic and dreary watch. A few words were exchanged, then the motor started off towards other ruins and silence fell on the scene again. Silence, yes, for the dull and distant rumbling of the guns becomes so habitual that it is heard no longer.

What gave the Belgian front its peculiar character was the manner in which the army had been obliged to construct its defence works. Because of the very high water table in that part of Flanders trenches could not be dug even at the height of summer; at a depth of 20 inches the spade sank into muddy ooze. The works therefore had to be made above ground level, by means of what the British Army called 'box parapets' of timber and sandbags; but these could not be too conspicuous, since in that bare plain there were no features of any kind to offer cover. This difficulty was solved by the Belgian Army by dint of ingenuity and patience. De Marès again:

I began in Nieuport. The little town that used to doze lazily at the mouth of the Yser, behind its pretty silted-up harbour, is now only a heap of rubbish. The bulbous steeple of its church is lying level with the ground; so is the handsome belfry of the Hall, and that massy tower of the Templars that seemed built to defy the hands of time. This is what the soldiers call 'the Water Sector', and the name is very well chosen. From Nieuport to Diksmuide stretches the even sheet of the vast flood.

By flooding the fields of Flanders the Belgians made most of the few roads almost invisible. It stopped the German invasion, and made it difficult for enemy reconnaissance pilots to read their pre-war maps, but their Allied comrades did not envy the Belgian troops serving on this sector of the front. They suffered badly from foot-rot and other disorders associated with perpetual dampness, and these were not simply discomforts: long exposure to such conditions could be crippling, and caused fatal bronchial diseases. (Langley Collection, Antwerp)

(continued on page 33)

GENERAL STAFF
1: Lieutenant-General Leman, 1914
2: HM King Albert I, 1915–18
3: Captain, General Staff, late 1914

F. Courcelle

A

INFANTRY, 1914

1 & 2: Corporal and private, 5th Line
Infantry, August

3: Private, Carabiniers, August

4: Private, Grenadiers, August

5: Infantryman, September

B

CAVALRY, 1914-15
1: Trooper, 1st Guides
2: Trooper, 2nd Lancers
3: Trooper, 1st Chasseurs à cheval

C

CAVALRY OFFICERS, 1914–15
1: Second Lieutenant, 1st Chasseurs à cheval
2: Captain, Guides
3: Colonel, 2nd Lancers

P. Courcelle

D

OFFICERS OF FOOT BRANCHES, 1914–18
1: Lieutenant, Line infantry, summer 1914
2: Subaltern officer, Line infantry, 1915
3: Captain, Grenadiers, summer 1916
4: Officer, all branches, 1916–18

E

F

G

INFANTRYMEN, 1916–18
1: Infantryman, winter 1918
2: Infantryman on patrol, Yser front, 1917
3: Scout-sniper, 1916–18
4: Cyclist, 4th Division, late 1918

P. Courcelle

H

Its wavelets are swept up by the breeze and die away at the foot of the embankment, and on raising one's head above the parapet one sees in front, as far as the eye can reach, nothing but grey sheet of water, from which small, reed-grown mud islands emerge here and there. Some of them have been turned into listening posts, and may be visited by means of light bridges or rafts; those are the 'water posts'. Can we imagine the lives led by the sentries on duty there, in solitude and in twilight, and during interminable nights?

As for the rampart itself – for it is a rampart, and not a trench – it is built of sandbags, of interwoven boughs, of gabions like those of Vauban's time, and it is as strong and comfortable as possible. Rising several metres above the level of the inundation, it is

broad enough to cover safe shelters dug at its base for the men to spend the night and brave all bombardments. On no other point along the front is such an impression of security to be enjoyed. But the loneliness!

All along the Yser, from Nieuport to Diksmuide, the flood kept the enemy at a distance; the German and Belgian lines were mostly separated by an interval of up to 3,000 yards, but near the German-held ruins of Diksmuide the trenches nearly touched, converging to about 10 yards apart. The sniping was uninterrupted, but neither side ever attempted a serious infantry action on any scale above occasional raids on each other's outposts.

Further south, towards Ypres, the country became somewhat less waterlogged, without changing its appearance of a devastated garden in which concealed defences had been constructed. Not a single village in what remained of unoccupied Belgium was wholly spared by the bombardment, and this strip of territory was nothing but an entrenched camp. De Marés on the 'empty battlefield':

Unless one knows the front intimately one cannot discover the trenches, the saps, the ammunition dumps or the batteries. The uninitiated might wander about the country for kilometres

Between June 1915 and September 1918 no major offensives took place on the Yser front. Service here was a constant fight against the water, but also against German snipers; reconnaissance patrols roamed the labyrinth of small islets rising above flood level to watch out for the enemy, and there were frequent small-scale clashes. (*N'oublions jamais*)

without seeing anyone but a few men of fatigue parties following the roads, and without suspecting that he is surrounded by thousands of watchful eyes – that below some harmless-looking mound of earth there is a battery, a command post connected by telephone with the headquarters of the sector, and that on the first alarm an infernal fire might in a few seconds be concentrated on the threatened point.

Between 6 and 18 March 1918 the Belgians flooded some further sectors where their defences were on the verge of collapse, at Riegersvliet and Oud-Stuyvekenskerke, in order to maintain their advantage. Only days later, the great German spring offensive of 1918 was to show that the Belgian Army was capable of taking a more active part in the climactic campaigns of the war.

LIBERATION

In January 1918 the brigade-level headquarters within the divisions was discontinued. The infantry component of each of the 'army divisions' was thereafter organized as 2 'infantry divisions'. A single cavalry division now comprised: 3 cavalry brigades each of 2 regiments; 2 cyclist battalions, 1 armoured car group, 3 batteries of 75mm guns, an engineer company and a platoon of cyclist-telegraphists. In total the Belgian Army then had a field strength of about 170,000 enlisted men and 5,700 officers, with 38,000 horses, and 850 artillery pieces (excluding trench mortars); an additional 30,000 men were employed in workshops, hospitals and other rear facilities.

The *Kaiserschlacht*, March–July 1918

While Operation 'Michael', the first offensive of Gen Ludendorff's final gamble, was driving deeply into the sectors of the British Third and Fifth Armies between Arras and Amiens during the last week of March 1918, preparations were also underway for a right flank offensive in Flanders. This Operation 'Georgette' was to be launched by the German Sixth Army on 9 April, striking the British Second Army between La Bassée and Armentières and thrusting north-west across the valley of the river Lys towards the important rail centre of Hazebrouck; the following day the German Fourth Army was to join the attack further north, towards the Messines Ridge south-east of Ypres. Success here might open a path towards the vital ports of Dunkirk and Calais, outflanking the whole Flanders front with incalculable consequences.

When this battle of the Lys started on 9 April, Gen von Quast's Sixth Army made rapid progress, punching up to 3½ miles west on a broad front and reaching the Lys at Estaires. When Gen von Arnim's Fourth joined in on 10 April it captured Ploegsteert, Messines village and Hollebeke; the British were compelled to abandon Armentières, and on the 12th began pulling west out of the Passchendaele salient captured with such agony in

A reconnaissance team returning from the flooded No Man's Land. From October 1915 onwards rubber boots were issued; the thigh-length waders (left) were made by the American 'US Rubber Cy and associated Companies'. Instead of Adrian helmets these two infantrymen wear the tasselled sidecap. The soldier on the right wears a rubberized jacket – a prized item held as trench stores, for issue to soldiers who had to go on reconnaissance. He also has a waist belt incorporating the strapped Argentine ammunition pouches, procured and locally copied in 1915 when leather started to become too scarce to continue production of the large Belgian belly-pouch. See also Plate H2. (*N'oublions jamais*)

From 1915 onwards, with the front stabilized and the floods hindering their use, four batteries of these Belgian 'auto-canons' (armoured cars) were sent to Russia at the request of the Tsar. The 1917 Bolshevik Revolution forced the Belgian government to withdraw them, via the United States and Britain; all remaining cars and equipment were destroyed before embarking. Their numbers never exceeded 350 men, and their participation on the Russian front was more symbolic than useful. The men sailed for Russia with specially made leather coats; after their arrival they adopted some Russian uniforms and equipment. (Langley Collection, Antwerp)

autumn 1917. On 14 April, Marshal Foch was given supreme command over the Allied armies and began shifting reserves, bringing French reinforcements up to this front to relieve battered Second Army divisions, but south of Ypres the British were still being driven back and the Germans approached Dranouter, Kemmel and St Eloi. A major German assault was then launched north of the town, driving south-westwards from the Houthulst Forest towards Poperinghe to encircle Ypres. Here they were resisted by the Belgian right wing formations, the 3rd, 4th and 9th Infantry Divisions. On a German prisoner the Belgians found an order of attack which included the words 'The Belgians are not used to being attacked in force; success is certain. They will be overthrown before they know where they are.'

On 17 April, after the kind of short but violent artillery preparation that they employed throughout the spring offensive, three German infantry divisions attacked near Merkem down the axis of a road towards Poperinghe; three more waited in the second line close to the Houthulst Forest, while a seventh was in rear reserve. The front-line units advanced quickly, with an apparent contempt for any dangers that might threaten their right wing. The first Belgian outposts near the road were swept away or submerged, but stubborn hand-to-hand fighting then delayed the enemy's march. By noon the Germans had reached the Belgian support line, but there they were stopped by the Belgian artillery playing on both their assault elements and their reserves. The decisive moment came when Belgian infantry advanced from their support trenches, and began to recapture lost ground behind a moving barrage. Caught between barrages in front and behind, the German units wavered – the formations assigned to Operation 'Georgette' were not storm troops but tired 'trench divisions'. Battalions broke, and the fighting degenerated into a number of smaller local battles. By 8pm the Belgians had recovered all the lost ground and taken more than 800 prisoners; the Belgian Army had shown that it could play its part in offensive operations as well as holding trenches. (Marshal Foch, the generalissimo of the western Allies, visited Belgian GHQ on 23 May, and in King Albert's presence conferred decorations on officers and men who had distinguished themselves in this battle of Merkem.)

On 19 April, the British Gen Plumer had to tighten the perimeter of the Ypres salient still further, and the Germans captured Bailleul. On the 25th, the German Alpine Corps drove French troops off Mount Kemmel, a 500-foot hill, which counts as a 'mountain' in Flanders. Yet although this feature dominated the Ypres salient from the south-west,

Training in the dunes near the North Sea, winter 1916–17. The appearance of the Belgian infantryman who would take part in the liberation campaign of 1918 had changed drastically since 1915, and at any distance he resembled a soldier of the French Colonial and Moroccan divisions. These troops wear M1915 Adrian helmets with cloth covers; under magnification they can be seen to carry slung M2 gasmasks, and their cartridge pouches are a mixture ranging from the old M1896 pattern to the mid-war Argentine type. (RMA, Brussels)

Grenadiers going from Roulers towards Loo for training in October 1916. (RMA, Brussels)

that German success was their last of the campaign; a further thrust at the British and French lines on 29 April achieved little, and that night Gen Ludendorff halted his Flanders offensive on a line through Loker, Clytte and Voormezele to Zillebeke and up to the east of Merkem. Like all the other phases of the Kaiserschlacht, it ran out of impetus, supplies and resolve, and in July the Allies gathered themselves to strike back. The counter-offensive was launched from the Marne on 18 July, and during August the balance turned decisively against the Germans, opening the way in the north for the liberation of Belgium.

The counter-offensive, September–November 1918

Belgian involvement intensified from September onwards. The Belgian Army now comprised 12 of the new infantry divisions or some 170,000 men; since the Belgian constitution dictated that only its sovereign could lead it, on 7 September King Albert I was appointed by Foch as commander of the Flanders Army Group, seconded by the French Gen Degoutte acting as chief of staff. Under their orders were Gen Gillain (Belgian Army), Gen Plumer (British Second Army) and Gen de Boissoudy (French Sixth Army). The outline of their operational plan to recapture territory to the north of the Lys was first of all to take control of the sector between the Ypres–Comines canal and the Clercken Ridge, before advancing towards Bruges and Courtrai. The Belgian troops occupied a front up to the Zonnebeke–Ypres road near the Bellewaerdebeeke.

From 28 to 30 September ten of the 12 Belgian divisions were engaged in the battle for the 'ridges' of Flanders, supported on their right by British Second Army and some elements from the French reserve. The first phase was an attack to take the Houthulst Forest and the ridge from Houthulst to Stadenberg, Westroosebeke, Passchendaele and Broodseinde. The second bound aimed to cross the marshy region between Diksmuide and Lake Blankaart, taking the ridge linking Essene and Clercken by an enveloping manoeuvre in order to recapture Diksmuide. On the night of 27/28 September, following a preparatory bombardment, the Belgian divisions broke through German lines, submerged their rear artillery batteries and pushed the front line back by up to 11 miles, with an average of nearly 4 miles along its entire length. The Houthulst Forest, Langemark and Poelkapelle were captured by 9th Division, Passchendaele by troops of 6th and 12th Divisions, Zonnebeke and Broodseinde by the 17th Line Infantry from 8th Division; in one day the Belgians took 150 guns and about 6,000 prisoners. On 29 September the advance continued, taking Diksmuide and the Essene ridge, reaching the

road from Roulers to Menin, and finishing by snuffing out the last German resistance in Westroosebeke. The next day and during the first days of October, with support from the French the Belgians attacked the line between Zarren and Hooglede-Roulers, forcing the Germans to retreat along more than 8 miles.

After a pause from 2 to 14 October, between the 14th and 30th the King of the Belgians launched the second phase of his Flanders offensive; now referred to as the battle of Thourout-Thielt, this was a joint Franco-Belgian operation combining two army corps with French tank support. To the north, one Belgian force was to capture the Handzaeme Canal and drive on to Thourout, while to the south another formation was to breach the front between Roulers and Ledeghem and cover the Army's right flank on the Lys. At dawn on 14 October, following artillery preparation, the attack was launched with naval gunfire support from the British Royal Navy. In hard fighting the French infantry reached the Roulers–Thourout road, attacking the Beveren sector further to the south and linking up with the Belgian assault in the north, allowing them to take the Handzaeme sector and the village of Cortemarck. To the south of Roulers the Belgians advanced 5 miles, taking Rumbeke and reaching the outskirts of Iseghem and Lendelede. On the evening of that same day, taking advantage of the rapid progress against German forces that were now in retreat, Belgian troops stationed along the flooded Diksmuide-Nieuport front advanced and reached the Yser on 16 October, joining up with British troops. The following day the Germans withdrew eastwards; the Belgian Army reached Ostend and the outskirts of Bruges, while the French were at the gates of Thielt. The battle of Flanders was over.

The Germans concentrated on the Lys and on the Deinze-Bruges canal put up fierce resistance against a Franco-Belgian attack on their lines from 20 October onwards. Things started to get moving again during the battle of the Lys between 31 October and 3 November, when Allied troops succeeded in crossing the river and advanced towards the Scheldt, up-river from Ghent. The Belgians gained a foothold on the east bank of the Lys and took charge of the Terneuzen section of the canal, reaching the western outskirts of Ghent to meet up with the French on the Scheldt to the south of Eecke. They remained in positions along this line Terneuzen-Ghent-Mons until the signing of the Armistice on 11 November brought the war to an end after 1,568 days.

In the final offensive to liberate their violated country the Belgian Army had paid a high price; between 4 October and 11 November 1918 it had lost more than one-fifth of its fighting strength in casualties – one-third of all the losses it sustained throughout the whole war. In the course of the conflict Belgium lost some 44,000 servicemen killed in action or dead of wounds or sickness; about 9,000 civilians also lost their lives, two-thirds of them during the German invasion of summer 1914. While these numbers were only a fraction of the millions of dead and

Belgian troops entering Aachen (Aken, Aix-la-Chapelle) in 1918. Following the Armistice it was agreed that Belgian forces were to occupy part of the German territory between the Belgian border and the Rhine, as well as four bridgeheads across the river in Germany, until 1923. (Oil painting by Alfred Bastien; RMA, Brussels)

wounded suffered by the French and British forces, they were significant for a population the size of Belgium's. This was all the more true given the high proportion of men of military age who had been trapped by the swift German occupation of 1914, and the fact that the Belgian Army had not been thrown into any of the massively costly French and British offensives of the mid-war years.

After the Great War the Treaty of Versailles awarded important war reparations to Belgium, to whose territory the cantons of Eupen, St Vith and Malmedy were added.

THE BELGIAN AIR FORCE

Belgian military aviation dated back to the first decade of the century when the Army established a balloon unit. Aircraft were first acquired in 1911, and in March that year the first airfield was inaugurated at Brasschaet, Antwerp. In 1913 the *Compagnie des Aviateurs* was created with four sections. At the outbreak of the war this small unit had a handful of Belgian-made Farman biplanes; from 4 August 1914 these made reconnaissance flights and in the early weeks they also 'bombed' invading German troops with iron darts. A number of civilian aviators enlisted, bringing their own machines to strengthen the air arm; among several pre-war celebrities to do so were the motorcycle champion Jan Olieslagers and his brothers, Henri Crombez, Tyck and De Caters. The French supplied extra aircraft and personnel, creating a mixed-nationality squadron and even mixed-nationality crews.

The stabilization of the front permitted the air arm – from 1915, the *Aviation Militaire Belge* – to reorganize on a war footing. A rear base with a depot for the repair and reception of aircraft was established in France at Calais Beaumarais with a flying school at Étampes, and operational airfields at Houtem and Koksijde in Belgium; Maj Nelis, one of the first Belgian military pilots, commanded the Calais depot throughout the war. Early in 1915 the air arm received its first Voisins from the French, and cameras for air-to-ground photography; aircraft also began to be fitted with bomb racks and machine guns. The first Nieuport single-seater 'scouts' were delivered in June 1915, but it was only on 26 August that the first true fighter mission was flown, by Lt Crombez. By early 1916 the air arm consisted of six squadrons (*escadrilles*). Single-seat fighters were not grouped in separate units from reconnaissance and bombing machines for some time, but operated with 1st, 2nd, 5th and 9th Squadrons.

The procurement of aircraft was a constant problem, and despite the modest overall numbers the inventory was extremely varied. Various marks of Farmans were employed alongside the British BE2c, RE8, Sopwith 1½-Strutter and Pup, and eventually the Camel. French types included Voisins, the Nieuport 10, 11, 17 and 23, the SPAD 7 and 11, Hanriot HD-1 and Breguet 14.

The leading Belgian air ace, Willy Coppens, was the greatest destroyer of observation balloons in the world; these heavily-protected targets counted for 35 of his 37 aerial victories. A former Grenadier who joined the air arm in September 1915, he started operations flying the

A Belgian pilot and his Farman MF11 'pusher'; Fernand Jacquet scored his first aerial victories from point-blank range while flying a two-seater Farman. This officer gives a good idea of the flying kit of a military airman early in the war: a protective leather crash-helmet, thick clothing topped with a stout leather jacket buttoned and belted, and high leather boots. Some airmen of the Belgian Army's reconnaissance squadrons achieved advanced skills in aerial photography. (Nelsons; Langley Collection, Antwerp)

BE2c and Sopwith 1½-Strutter with 6th Squadron. In mid-July 1917 he transferred to Capt Fernand Jacquet's 1st (Fighter) Sqn, flying Nieuport 17s alongside the aces Lt André de Meulemeester and Sgt Jan Olieslagers; Coppens later preferred to fly the Hanriot HD-1, which was delivered from August 1917. De Meulemeester (11 confirmed victories, but probably 28) also flew the Hanriot, with 1st and 9th Squadrons. Olieslagers flew Nieuports, Hanriots, and from September 1917 Sopwith Camels with 2nd and 1st Sqns; although his official score was 6 (he never claimed any himself) comrades would testify that he shot down many more behind German lines where ground confirmation was seldom possible. The third-ranking of Belgium's five official aces was 2nd Lt Edmond Thieffry, who achieved the first of his 10 confirmed victories on 15 March 1917 flying a Nieuport with 5th Sqn, which later received SPADs.

On 4 May 1917 a daring mission was flown by Henri Crombez and Louis Robin from 6th Sqn, who flew deep behind enemy lines to drop a Belgian flag over occupied Brussels. Another famous flight was made by King Albert, who on 6 July 1917 was taken over the front in a Sopwith 1½-Strutter in order to observe the situation for himself – thus becoming almost certainly the only reigning monarch in the world ever to fly a military combat mission. That month the small Aviation Militaire was putting up an average of 120 sorties each day.

On 23 December 1917 the Franco-Belgian Escadrille left the Belgian sector to become a fully French unit, Escadrille C74. Early in 1918 the Belgian airmen took responsibility for the sector west of the Ostend–Vijfwegen railway tracks, and for first time air-ground co-operation and communication were professionally organized. Some Belgian aircrews specialized in air-to-ground photography; an officer named Jaumotte developed such expertise that British and French headquarters often asked specifically for pictures taken by him personally.

February 1918 saw the formation of *Groupe de Chasse Jacquet* (Fighter Group Jacquet). Major Fernand Jacquet, Belgium's fourth ranking ace (7 confirmed kills) now commanded a concentration of Belgian fighters to provide protection for observation aircraft and ground units and to fly air-superiority patrols. Pilots including Coppens, Olieslagers and Demeulemeester flew Hanriots, SPAD 7s and Camels with this group, which became operational just before the German March offensive. Just before the troops left their trenches on 28 September for the Flanders counter-offensive, Belgian Breguet 14s and SPAD 11s took off to support the infantry. Some aircraft were employed in bombing and strafing German positions, and others dropped munitions and supplies to the advancing troops.

On 17 October 1918 pilots of the Groupe Jacquet landed in Ostend, the first members of the Belgian Army to enter the town after four years of German occupation.

THE APPEARANCE OF THE BELGIAN INFANTRYMAN

Some specifics will be found in the Plate Commentaries at the end of this text; what follows is a general explanation.

On mobilization, 1914

Unlike the French or Germans the Belgians had not experienced the instructive shock of wars in the late 19th century, and the soldier's general appearance had changed little since the major reforms of 1853 (privates even retained the traditional short infantry sabre until 1899). The latest advances had been studied, but not urgently, since the government always considered Belgium's neutrality a guarantee of peace; by 1914 the army only had some 100 machine guns, and uniform trials in 1911 and 1914 did not change the general appearance of the rank and file before the opening of hostilities. Reports by inspecting officers were rarely complimentary, and the Belgian soldier was sometimes labelled as indisciplined and careless. Not too concerned about his appearance, he considered it normal to deform any items that he judged too uncomfortable: 'When in town the soldiers moved around in a dirty and slovenly manner. On seeing an officer approaching they would move in such way as not to have to salute him. One could see them walking with chin on chest, feet gliding over the ground. Infantrymen, always without arms or belts, wearing their greatcoat and awful headgear, had a wretched look. The officers were no better, and on parade their multifarious uniforms gave an impression of a flock without consistency.'

During the battles for Antwerp and on the Yser in September–October 1914 the poor appearance of the troops simply had to be ignored. The winds from the sea obliged the soldiers to keep their hands in their pockets, turn up the greatcoat collar and let its skirts flap unbuttoned. The army that halted at Diksmuide was motley and ragged, and it included volunteers who had not yet been issued any kind of uniform and who had to fight in civilian clothes. The Germans, convinced of the presence of partisans in Belgium, accused them of being *francs-tireurs*, and on those grounds sought to justify the horrors they committed on the Herve plateau, in the south

Men of the 3rd Line Infantry Regiment resting in Brussels after the battle of Louvain, August 1914. Their uniforms are complete and in good order, and the soldiers still look determined and optimistic. They wear the M1868/1883 infantry field cap copied from the German model, with the red/yellow/black national cockade above the dark blue regimental number. The man standing at right still has the red pompon and a white-painted regimental number on the oilskin cover of his shako. In the foreground, note the dark blue trouser piping and the leather M1891 anklets. See Plate B1. (RMA, Brussels))

of Luxembourg, at Leuven (Louvain), Dinant, Aarschot, Dendermonde and other places.

The fortress troops were disproportionately numerous when compared to the relatively low strength of the Field Army. In theory they were drawn from the older men, but even so their age was not over 35 years. Considering the poor leadership they received these soldiers performed well during the attacks on the forts. The gunners, usually conscripted from the region of the fortresses where they would serve, obtained good results thanks to their familiar knowledge of the countryside, but the crushing technological superiority of the German artillery made their task hopeless. They usually wore the same uniforms as they had when serving in the Field Army as younger men; the main differences were a shako with a foul-weather cover (without insignia) instead of the artillery *talpack*, and obsolete equipment such as the old single-shot Albini rifle. Only small details permitted exact identification: the Fortress Artillery wore buttons with crossed cannon, and brass cyphers on the shoulder straps ('L', 'N' or 'A' for Liège, Namur or Antwerp).

The *Carabiniers-Cyclistes* battalion of the Belgian Cavalry Division were armed with Danish Madsen light machine guns in addition to their rifles. Often operating in conjunction with armoured cars, they took a heavy toll of German cavalrymen, especially in the successful engagement at Haelen on 12 August 1914. Note the distinctive beaked appearance of their tapered caps, which bore yellow distinctions and bugle-horn badges. The cycle could be folded for carriage on the back when necessary. (RMA, Brussels)

On the Yser, 1914–15 (blue uniform)

The British and French troops who served in Flanders complained of the ever-present dampness and of having to build 'box parapets', but they did not have to build up their positions simply to avoid drowning, as was the case in the Belgian sector in the extreme north. The Belgian soldiers' collective nickname – the equivalent of *poilu*, Tommy, *Landser* and Doughboy – was '*Jas*', the Flemish word for coat. This was little appreciated by the soldiers in the line, since they lacked nearly all basic necessities including weatherproof coats, and there was rarely any opportunity for them to dry out their constantly soaked and muddy uniforms.

In the retreat from Antwerp much of the clothing and other stores had been left to the enemy. One volunteer recalled that in his unit of some 200 men no two of them were dressed alike. Some wore yellow or black boots, wooden clogs or even slippers; the trousers were of every possible colour, including some that were nameless in any language. There was such a profusion of different jackets or tunics that it was impossible to list them all: old-model Lancer jackets, Carabinier tunics, jackets turned inside out, others modified by the user or by some would-be tailor he had met along the road.

In the hope of countering this chaos the Army staff tried to furnish the soldiers with clothing that was at least practical, even if no uniformity could be achieved. An order of 3 September 1914 established a new universal field cap for the entire army, modelled on that already in use by the Engineers. This soft-topped dark blue or dark green képi had a folding double flap that could be turned down to cover the cheeks and

Lancers passing infantry of the *Garde Civique* near Louvain, August 1914. Once mobilized, the Civil Guard passed from the control of the Interior Ministry to that of the War Ministry; their second-line defence duties involved guarding depots, railway stations and lines of communiction. From 23 August 1914 onwards some units, together with gendarmes, volunteers and urban Civil Guards were united into a formation commanded by LtGen Clooten, which saw action in East and West Flanders. (Nelsons; Langley Collection, Antwerp)

neck and fastened in front by two black buttons; piping in distinctive branch colour was supposed to be sewn around the crown seam. Made in large numbers, this headgear was not in fact worn until after the first battle for the Yser, thus its popular name of 'Yser cap'. Since the leather peak was of poor quality and the cloth was not water-resistant it soon made a poor impression, and was abandoned with the later introduction of the khaki uniform.

Progress in resupplying the Army was slow and any immediate help that could be provided was gratefully received. With the national territory almost completely occupied by the enemy, contracts were given to numerous factories in France and Great Britain. A supply service was organized, and while a network of small repair workshops were improvised locally, Rouen and Rennes became the principal supply centres for the Belgian Army. In November 1914 the French offered a wide variety of items in generous quantities, all made to French patterns for the sake of speed. The small stocks brought out of Antwerp were exclusively reserved for the Field Army, but were rapidly used up. Aggravating these problems was the fact that Belgian uniforms were more complicated to make than French ones; for instance, one workshop was able to make 11 French greatcoats in the time it took to produce seven Belgian ones. Shortages of both cloth and funds dictated the alteration of some uniform patterns. Greatcoats were simplified in cut, and since the fabric used was that woven for civilian overcoats the shortages resulted in a variety of colours and qualities being worn. Like the French Army of 1914–15 the Belgians received much clothing made in corduroy, including trousers in a brownish-red shade called 'wine-red'.

The M1891 leather anklets were still made but in insufficient numbers and of thinner hide; they finally became so rare that hardly a soldier was seen without his trousers either tucked into his woollen socks or confined by various cloth ankle-wrappings. Since the other Allied armies used puttees it was natural for the Belgians to do likewise. Officially only the Gendarmerie was allowed, during the rest of the war, to wear black puttees, but in fact officers at the front and even at the instruction centres closed their eyes to a great diversity of dress. Knapsacks were only used behind the lines; where possible, replacements were modelled on the French proofed canvas type, but most were still made from the old unshaven hide, though in simplified form for speed and economy. Alongside French and Canadian troops, Belgian Carabiniers and Grenadiers suffered the first poison-gas casualties at Steenstrate on 23 and 24 April 1915, and during the following weeks the first, very basic anti-gas masks were distributed.

Arms came from Britain, where the Browning factories provided much-needed replacements for the Belgian Mausers, and weapons captured by the Allies were passed on to the Belgians; because its ammunition was available in quantity the French 8mm Lebel M1886/93 also came into service. As already noted, the Belgian artillery was supplied at first with

French 75mm shells, but these proved too powerful for their Krupps and soon wore them out; France then undertook a complete re-equipment of the branch.

On the Yser, 1915–18 (khaki uniform)

Even in simplified form the old blue uniform was no longer acceptable, and stocks of dark-blue cloth were not inexhaustible. From July 1915 onwards the silhouette of the Belgian soldier began to change, ending finally in a strange combination of French and British styles.

Numerous committees were formed to organize the procurement of better-quality uniforms and equipment, and Belgian industrialists who had sought refuge in France played a prominent role. Baron Empain, a wealthy engineer, financier and industrialist, had contacts in the USA, France and Italy, and C. Barbanson and Duesbery of the Simonis company were asked to find khaki cloth to make some 100,000–250,000 uniforms for the Belgian Army. The need to start production quickly caused some carelessness over quality control; for instance, of 18,000 greatcoats made by the Elders company 3,600 were judged unacceptable. Slowly the situation improved, but even a standardized shade of khaki was not achieved. One of the orders for khaki cloth went to Italy for 950,000 metres of material of a shade described as 'dark dead leaf'. When 25,000 metres had been made the order was cancelled in favour of the khaki shade used by the British, which allowed quick production in large quantities by Italian and American companies as well as British manufacturers. The 25,000 metres of 'dead leaf' cloth already delivered was nevertheless finally used to make up Belgian uniforms.

The khaki uniform was introduced in the course of spring 1915, and the first soldiers dressed in khaki were sent to the front around July of that year. The first uniform for the infantry consisted of a four-pocket British-type tunic but made in cotton, and a straight pair of trousers in the same material, while the cavalry, artillery and cyclists used riding breeches. A cap of the British type with a soft crown and a cloth-covered peak (vizor) was worn continuously in the front lines until the French

Light infantry officers of the *Chasseurs à pied*, resting in October 1914. Both the shako and the M1900 képi were usually worn in the field with a waxed or oiled campaign cover, and the shako pompon was usually removed or lost. Note the high, rigid leather gaiters. Here, the regulation M1897 officers' greatcoat is seen next to an officer's rubberized (*caoutchouc*) coat – partly visible at left centre – at that date a tolerated private-purchase item, which would soon be much more widely used on the Yser front. (RMA, Brussels)

Winter on the Yser front. Following the British example, men who had to stand guard were issued with sheepskin jerkins or watchcoats held around the waist by a simple leather belt; nobody bothered whether the hide or the fleece was worn outermost. During the weary years in Flanders a commerce naturally grew up between the Belgians and neighbouring Allied troops. The most desirable French goods were furs, and the Belgians were known for fine quality bread. British leather jerkins and trenchcoats were popular, and – though it is widely believed that only a true Briton can relish eating 'Bovril' on bread – the Belgians did admit that with hot water it made a tasty and warming *bouillon*. (Author's collection))

Adrian M1915 steel helmet replaced it in November of that year. The first shipments, though bearing the Belgian national lion's-mask insignia, were factory-painted in *bleu-horizon*; later they were delivered painted in khaki. Thereafter the British soft cap was only permitted to be worn behind the front lines; it was supposed to have crown piping in branch colours, and bore the national cockade above a unit number or badge. It was replaced during winter 1916/17 with the khaki sidecap with piping and frontal tassel in branch colour.

At the end of October 1915 a winter woollen version of the khaki tunic and trousers were distributed; according to the recollection of the Belgian veteran Antoon Visser (101 years of age in 1999), these first deliveries of straight wool trousers were in fact former red French trousers re-dyed khaki. The mounted and cyclist branches again received riding breeches and high leather leggings. Quantities of actual British Army uniform were also delivered; later, United States Army M1917 tunics, trousers and greatcoats were also issued, these too being modified for Belgian Army use with Belgian lion buttons, branch-colour collar patches and piped shoulder straps. Tunic collar patches identified branch of service by base colour and contrasting piping and in some cases badges, and shoulder straps bore the same, or regimental or divisional numbers in Arabic and Roman form respectively. In all these details, the actual practice often differed from the regulations under the pressures of war.

Officers' tunics were of British cut except for the standing collar, which bore the same rank stars and bars as the old pre-1913 tunic on new coloured and piped patches; shoulder straps, Polish cuffs, trousers, and breeches (of paler khaki material) might have branch-colour piping. British-style officers' service caps were supposed to have branch-colour crown piping, and bore the national cockade above the unit number or a badge; the sidecap had gold piping and tassel and a branch-colour band.

SELECT BIBLIOGRAPHY

De Schaepdrijver, S., *De Groote Oorlog: het koninkrijk België tijdens de Eerste Wereldoorlog – La Belgique et la Première Guerre mondiale* (Amsterdam & Bruxelles, 1997–2004)

Dubrunfaut, P. (dir), *Les armes à feu réglementaires belges depuis 1830* (Bruxelles, 1988)

Lefebvre, P. & J. Lorette (dir), *La Belgique et la Première Guerre mondiale – Bibliographie* (Bruxelles, 1987); Soupart, S. & P.A. Tallier, ibid, Vol 2 (2000)

Lierneux, P. & F. Nicolas, Belgian uniform articles published in *Militaria Magazine* (Paris), Nos. 66, 71, 160, 175, 178, 217, 219, 221 & 257

PLATE COMMENTARIES

A: GENERAL STAFF

A1: Lieutenant-General Leman, 1914

The full dress dark blue uniform, piped crimson, was invariably worn by general officers at the beginning of the war; it is complete with full dress shoulder knots, but here with ankle boots and rigid leather gaiters for service dress. The three vertical gold lace quarter-stripes on the képi identified all general officers, the five rings around it lieutenant-generals.

A2: HM King Albert I, 1915–18

The King of the Belgians wears the khaki uniform, and the khaki-painted Adrian helmet with the national lion-mask insignia, which were standard in 1915–18. Apart from the standing collar and pointed 'Polish' cuffs the cut of the officer's M1915 uniform closely resembled the contemporary British pattern. The crimson-piped black velvet collar patches of Belgian general officers display the two gold bars and three stars of lieutenant-general's rank, the most senior in the Belgian Army, and the General Staff *foudre* insignia – a stylized bundle of lightning-bolts. The rank and piping are also seen on the khaki shoulder straps, and piping on the cuffs.

A3: Captain, General Staff corps, late 1914

This officer wears the dark green uniform of officers attached to the General Staff. The M1892 tunic has added breast pockets, and photos and surviving uniforms show the use of M1914 full dress shoulder straps; campaign uniform was to some extent a matter of personal taste, since it was covered by no strict regulations. Company officers' collars bore one to three stars, here with the addition of the staff *foudre*. The chain is for attaching the sabre to an internal belt; and note the Nagant M1878 revolver.

B: INFANTRY, 1914

B1 & 2: Corporal and private, 5th Line Infantry, August

The impractical and easily-lost shako has a waxed or oiled rain-cover, a pompon (red for Line infantry, green for Chasseurs) and a regimental number, here '5'. The shako was often replaced with the more practical fatigue cap, a German-style 'pork pie' piped in Line infantry blue-grey and adorned with a national red/yellow/black cockade and the regimental number. The '*gros bleu*' double-breasted greatcoat, here the M1906 model (though older patterns were still in use) was worn in all seasons; it had two rows of six brass buttons, and the skirts buttoned back to free the legs for marching. Note that the flapped side pockets, rear vent and integral rear half-belt were also buttoned. The yellow corporal's stripes were worn on both forearms, as were the one and two gold stripes of two grades of sergeant; the single yellow stripe of senior private was worn on the left sleeve only. The grey-blue trousers were officially piped red, later changed to dark blue for less visibility, but in practice were usually unpiped; they were confined in M1891 leather ankle-gaiters. The double-breasted dark blue tunic worn under the greatcoat was piped down the front and around the pointed cuffs in blue-grey. The Chasseurs wore a dark green tunic piped yellow, and blue-grey trousers officially piped green.

The weapon was the Belgian Mauser rifle in 7.65mm with a five-round magazine, adopted in 1889. The M1896 equipment comprised a belt with a plain clipped-square brass plate; a large ventral cartridge pouch; a brownish-grey

Their characteristic hats made the Carabiniers one of the most popularly represented types of troops in the pre-war years. These images appeared in a French comparative study, *Sac au dos*, published in Paris in 1902; see Plate B3. (Author's collection)

'beggar's bag' haversack behind the right hip, to which was attached a 1-litre aluminium canteen in a cover of similar cloth; an entrenching tool and the M1884 bayonet, with black leather carrier and frog respectively. The M1896 knapsack was of German inspiration, of unshaven cowhide lined with cloth; the practice of carrying spare ammunition inside condemned the Belgian soldier to keep it with him at all times. The squad's black-painted 2.5-litre aluminium *marmite* is shown attached to the flap (**errata**: the rolled tent section illustrated is shown in error – experiments with this item had ceased by 1914). When the knapsack was worn the heavy ventral ammo pouch helped balance its weight; when it was dropped, the weight of the pouch became a problem.

B3: Private, Carabiniers, August

This elite unit is identified most obviously by the 'Corsican' hat, here in an oilskin cover. The greatcoat was supposedly green but was in practice black, earning them the German nickname of 'Black Devils'. The colour of the trousers was called 'Marengo-grey' and they were officially piped yellow, but in fact they varied from dark mouse-grey almost to black and were seldom piped. The Carabiniers' field equipment was of standard Line pattern; note that the belt buckle was often worn left of centre to bring the cartridge pouch more handily to the right. The Carabinier-Cyclists wore a tapered peaked field cap instead of the hat, with a yellow band and piping and a Carabinier bugle-horn badge.

B4: Private, Grenadiers, August

On campaign he wears the standard Line infantry uniform with the distinctions of this elite unit. The regulation fatigue cap is distinguished by a red band and piping and a cut-out dark blue grenade badge, and the greatcoat by red collar patches with brass grenades. (The dark blue tunic and trousers were supposed to be piped red, but the latter were usually plain 'Marengo-grey').

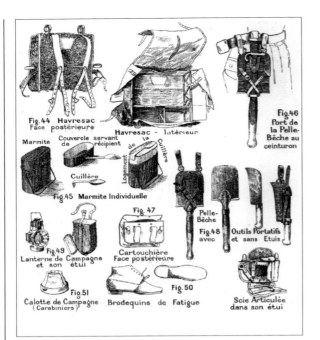

Fig.44 Havresac
Face postérieure
Havresac - Intérieur
Fig.46
Port de
la Pelle-
Bêche au
ceinturon
Marmite
Couvercle servant
de récipient
Logement de la
cuillère
Cuillère
Cuillère
Fig.45 Marmite Individuelle
Fig 47
Pelle-
Bêche
Fig.48
avec
Outils Portatifs
et sans Etuis
Fig.49
Lanterne de Campagne
et son étui
Cartouchière
Face postérieure
Fig.51
Calotte de Campagne
(Carabiniers)
Brodequins de Fatigue
Fig.50
Scie Articulée
dans son étui

Details of the M1896 infantry knapsack and equipment items, from *Sac au dos* (1902); they were still in use in 1914 – see Plate B2. Also shown at bottom left is the sharply-tapered field cap of the Carabiniers. The use of lightweight aluminium for some equipment items was one of the few modernizing reforms to Belgian uniforms and kit in the pre-war years. (Author's collection)

B5: Infantryman, September
Taken from a photograph, this soldier on the retreat to Antwerp has accomodated himself to the heat as best he can. His fatigue cap is worn inside out to make it less conspicuous and has an added cardboard peak or vizor. His greatcoat is worn wide open, with a large neckerchief, and the hanging pockets visible in the lining of the turned-back skirts probably hold cartridges.

C: CAVALRY, 1914–15
C1: Trooper, 1st Guides
These two elite regiments went to war in the dress of another age; if the bearskin *colback* (at least strippped of its plume) was soon discarded in favour of the *bonnet de police*, the green and red uniform lasted until mid-1915. The M1903 cavalry tunic is green with red facings and piping. The breeches had evolved since the 1860s into a sort of hybrid of breeches and leather-reinforced 'Lassalle'-style overalls. The horse furniture was M1863 pattern; the sabre carried at the saddle was a French M1822 modified in 1883, and the carbine the M1889 Belgian Mauser.
C2: Trooper, 2nd Lancers
This lancer wears a uniform essentially similar to that of the Guides but in branch colours of dark blue and grey-blue with regimental distinctions, here yellow (1st, red; 3rd & 5th, white; 4th, sky-blue). The black 'false *chapska*', made of card covered with oilskin, has been replaced with the *bonnet de police* laced and tasselled in the regimental colour; seam piping in the same colour is applied between the white stripes on the breeches. Note the lance pennon in national colours.
C3: Trooper, 1st Chasseurs à cheval
The uniform of these regiments generally followed those described above, but this branch wore a shako, with an oilskin cover for field use. The distinctive colours were red for the 1st & 4th Regiments and yellow for the 2nd.

D: CAVALRY OFFICERS, 1914–15
With no alternative (and doubtless with no great wish for one), Belgian cavalry officers went to war in their elegant peacetime *petites tenues*. The only concessions to field conditions were to replace the parade headgear with a képi or a *bonnet de police*, and their regimental dolmans had most of the gold or silver lace and loops replaced in black.
D1: Second Lieutenant, 1st Chasseurs à cheval
In the summer heat this *sous-lieutenant* has tucked a handkerchief beneath his M1900/1910 képi. His rank is indicated by the single Hungarian knot of bullion lace on the sleeves of his regimental dolman, with its otherwise black cords, loops and toggles. His sidearm is a French ordnance-issue revolver in its characteristic deep-shell holster.
D2: Captain, Guides
The laced and tasselled *bonnet de police* replaces the bearskin, but he too retains bullion Hungarian knots on his sleeves. His revolver is the Nagant M1878, and he also carries the sabre, mapcase and binoculars. His horse furniture would be the same as that for figure D3, apart from a green rolled cloak in place of the Lancer's dark blue.
D3: Colonel, 2nd Lancers
This field officer chooses to wear the comfortable M1914 tunic, modified with an integral cloth belt; this 'sporting' item is a practical alternative for his expensive and easily damaged dolman. The collar patches of field officers displayed a single vertical bar and one, two or three stars; this colonel also has the *foudre* showing that he is attached to the General Staff. The black-covered *chapska* was discarded after the first few days' fighting.

E: OFFICERS OF FOOT BRANCHES, 1914–18
E1: Lieutenant, Line infantry, summer 1914
A reconstruction from several surviving items, this lieutenant wears the képi and the single-breasted M1913 tunic, which displays his rank in the form of cuff-rings; it has laced three-button cuff flaps, and is piped in infantry blue-grey at the collar, cuffs and front edge. He chooses to wear the expensive but popular Bedford cord breeches with chamois leather reinforcement. Rigid leather leggings 'à la Manfield', worn over laced civilian boots, complete his outfit.
E2: Officer, Line infantry, 1915
Taken from a photograph, this subaltern – from his collar-patch star, a second lieutenant – is typical of the confusion of mixed items worn in the aftermath of the 1914–15 battles. He wears the famous 'Yser cap'; oddly, it seems to be piped in red, and bears an anachronistic two-bar rank insignia on the front – this practice was strictly forbidden. The tunic is the double-breasted M1914 with infantry grey-blue trim; note the piped false pocket flaps at the rear. The black corduroy trousers are confined in non-regulation leggings. His weapon is the popular .45cal Colt 1911 semi-automatic, and he carries the standard M1898 mapcase.

A Belgian Engineer officer, Lt Léopold Calberg (killed 16 July 1917) wearing the 1915 khaki uniform, complete with high rubber trench boots. Note the capacious bellows pockets of the British-style officer's tunic, but with its Belgian standing collar. The black collar patches, piped scarlet, bear the single gold star of his rank ahead of the antique helmet symbol of the Engineer branch. Either this, or a Roman divisional numeral, would normally be worn on the shoulder straps. Visible on his left upper sleeve are four of the gold diagonal stripes (gilt metal for officers) denoting front-line service: the first for a year, and subsequent awards for every additional six months, so Lt Calberg's show 2½ years' service. (*Nieuport 1914–1918*)

E3: Captain, Grenadiers, summer 1916

This officer wears a cotton lightweight version of the uniform '*à l'anglaise*' inspired by the 1902 service dress of British officers; note that in this case the six-button tunic has a stand-and-fall collar, with insignia pinned directly to the cloth. The cap displays the national cockade above a metal grenade, which is repeated in black cut-out cloth on the shoulder straps; both these and the cuffs are piped black. He too carries a Colt, and wears British-style Sam Browne belt equipment. The leggings were regulation; it was strictly forbidden for subalterns to wear puttees, although rear-echelon types sometimes sported them.

E4: Officer, all branches, 1916–18

This *sous-lieutenant* using a trench periscope has covered his Adrian helmet with sandbag cloth to kill reflections and soften its outline. This tunic is of classic Belgian cut with a high stand collar and pointed cuffs. The collar patches, piping and rank insignia preserved a link with the uniforms of 1914. The main branches were identified by, e.g: *Line infantry*, scarlet patches, piped royal blue; *Chasseurs á pied & Carabiniers*, green patches, yellow piping; *Guides*, crimson patches, green piping; *Lancers*, white patches, royal blue piping; *Chasseurs á cheval*, yellow patches, royal blue piping; *Artillery*, royal blue patches, scarlet piping; *Engineers*: black patches, scarlet piping; *Air corps*, sky-blue patches, scarlet piping. Shoulder straps might display unit or branch cyphers or insignia – e.g. the grenade or bugle-horn for elite heavy and light infantry, Arabic unit numbers, Roman divisional numbers, 'M' for machine-gunners, 'C' for horse artillery, 'O' or 'L' for heavy howitzer or gun units, an antique helmet symbol for engineers, etc. The *Aviation Militaire* displayed a gold winged 'A' badge on upper left sleeve and cap.

F–G: SOMEWHERE ON THE YSER FRONT, SEPTEMBER 1918

H: INFANTRYMEN, 1916–18

H1: Infantryman, winter 1918

The typical '*Jas*' of the last year of the war. In 1916–18 greatcoats were seen with one or two rows of drab-painted Belgian lion buttons, with or without vertical slash pockets above the flapped side-pockets; broad shoulder straps were fastened with a button at each end, and might be piped in branch-colour. Rank insignia for corporals and sergeants were worn on both sleeves: two red diagonals, one silver or gold, and two silver or gold with a knot in the top stripe. Equipment changed from black to brown leather during 1915; from 1917 this British-made Mills web equipment began to appear – note the US-type belt clasp. French gasmasks were carried in slung metal canisters.

H2: Infantryman on patrol, Yser front, 1917

He wears the *bonnet de police* with an infantry-scarlet tassel; it seems undersized, and note that he has added a chinstrap. The khaki tunic has branch-colour collar patches; over his trousers he wears a pair of the prized but hard-to-get rubberized fishing waders. Note the mid-war 'Argentine' pouches, so called even after they were mass-produced in Paris. He has a French bayonet and a *poignard*-style trench dagger, and only his canteen and haversack (hidden here) recall the 1914 Belgian equipment.

H3: Scout-sniper, 1916–18

Such specialists might wear a special vizored 'Queen Elizabeth' helmet to give extra concealment and protection during the few seconds when they might be exposed.

H4: Cyclist, 4th Division, late 1918

Note the shortened greatcoat with flapless pockets. Cyclists were issued the breeches and leggings of the mounted branches, worn here with blackened boots. This branch was the first to be issued the 'Argentine' pouches.

INDEX